Davey isn't Afraid of Goodbyes

A Story about Overcoming Separation Anxiety

Dr. Jonathan Kushnir
& Ram Kushnir

Illustrations by Nikola Aronová

Davey isn't Afraid of Goodbyes
A Story about Overcoming Separation Anxiety

Written By: Dr. Jonathan Kushnir, Ram Kushnir
Illustrations: Nikola Aronová

Printed in the United States of America
First Printing, 2024
ISBN: 9798334197053
Please visit us online for more information at:
https://cbtails.com

Introduction to the Reading Parent

Kids can naturally separate from their parents in situations like going to school, visiting friends, or using the bathroom. Most children feel secure being away from their parents by age 5, which is a significant growth step. However, some find it very hard, making each goodbye stressful for both the child and parents.

Children anxious about separation often feel very upset. If they're apart, they may think something terrible will happen to them or their parents. These kids only feel safe with a parent nearby and avoid being separated. This can negatively affect both children and parents. Kids might miss out on social activities and fun experiences. Parents often must stay close, limiting their daily routines and personal time.

This book shows how kids and parents can deal with separation fears calmly and effectively. It uses Cognitive Behavioral Therapy principles to address these concerns in a gentle, easy-to-understand way.

We hope that embedding these principles in the story will enable parents to introduce and implement them easily with their children. The principles described in this book are based on years of research and treatment in the field of child anxiety. We hope you find this book helpful. Enjoy reading!

Please note that this book is not a substitute for treatment by a qualified professional.

4

Once upon a time, in a small town by a lake, lived a curious boy named Davey. Davey loved playing along the lakeshore, where the water sparkled in the sunlight.

Davey had a great time in his little town.
What he loved most was being with his
parents. He explored the hills with his mom
and listened to his dad's funny stories.

In fact, he loved being with his parents so
much that it was almost impossible for him
to say goodbye, even for a moment.

When his parents were out of sight, he was always sure something terrible would happen. Scary thoughts went through his head. Thoughts like, "Will Mom and Dad be back soon? What if something happens to me before they return?!"

Davey also had unpleasant feelings in his body. His heart pounded, his belly ached, and he would sweat and sometimes shake. Everywhere Davey went, even to bed or the bathroom, he had to be sure his parents hadn't gone away.

"Daddy, Mommy, are you there?" he would ask repeatedly. And although this sometimes angered them, they always replied, "it's okay, sweetie. We're right here."

Mom and Dad didn't know how to help Davey, until something happened one cold morning when it was snowy and white outside.

It was "Snowman Morning." Every year, after the first snow fell, all the town's children got up early, climbed up Tabletop Hill without their parents, and built a big snowman together.

"I can't go," Davey said in a trembling voice. "If something bad happens on our way up, I'll be all by myself while you're away and unable to help." Mom smiled, "Do not worry, sweetie. If anything happens, we'll come immediately." Davey insisted, "What if something happens to YOU when I'm on the hill?"

"We'll be fine!" Said Davey's dad. "Go with your friends." "I can't!" Davey said, holding his mom's hand as tightly as he could. "I'm not going without you!"

Davey's parents were helpless. Davey was determined not to go, and they had no choice but to go home. As the family began walking back, they heard a familiar voice: "Hello there!" That was Dorothy's voice. Dorothy was Dad's schoolteacher and the wisest woman in town.

"I see little Davey cannot say goodbye!" Dorothy said. "Yes, that's right," Mom answered. "Even for a minute." And Dad added, "Davey really wants to say goodbye, but he can't, and we just don't know how to help him. We are so frustrated!"

Dorothy listened patiently and said, "When I was little, I too could not say goodbye on Snowman Morning." "You did!?" Davey asked. He couldn't imagine Dorothy scared of anything.

15

"Yes. You see, sometimes frightening, untrue thoughts pop into our heads. It is like someone's sitting in there, like a big bully, making up phony stories.

"Can we do anything about that bully?" Dad asked. Dorothy turned to Davey and said, "Let's start by giving him a name. What name would you like to give him?"

"Can I pick any name I want?" "Of course."
"Then I would like to name him... Tricksy."
"That's a great name," Dorothy said. "He
really does play tricks on our minds!"

"And we can get rid of Tricksy if we take small steps. With each little step, you will get used to being less and less with Mom and Dad." Davey nodded. "Now, let's get to work. I have some tasks for you," Dorothy smiled.

She gave the family a set of tasks and explained them carefully. "These tasks are stepping stones to your freedom. And I'm warning you: Tricksy will try to make them feel scary, but remember, whatever he says, they're just stories!"
"Thank you, Dorothy!" Davey and his parents said as they turned to go back home.

The next day, Mom said to Davey, "It's time for our first task." They went to the park and stood near a tall tree. Mom said, "Davey, stand with your back to me, and I will begin to walk away."

"As I walk further from the tree, you will stop hearing my footsteps. Your job is to stay here and hold out until I return." "OK, let's do it," Davey said, although he was scared.

Mom walked away until her footsteps faded in the distance. A few moments passed, and Davey began feeling hot and sweaty. Pretty soon, bad thoughts popped into his head.

Just as Davey was about to shout, he heard Mom's voice: "Well done! You've made it." She stood next to him, and he immediately felt better.

"OK, let's try again. Now, I will go for a longer time," Mom said. "Again, your job is to stay here and be strong." "I'm ready," Davey said. Mom's steps quietened as she walked away.

22

Davey held out nicely until, after a few moments, he heard a loud shout from somewhere in the park. "Something happened to Mom!" He immediately thought. His heart began pounding heavily. Davey held himself for a moment until he called, "Mom! Where are you??! Come back!"

23

Mom quickly returned and stood beside Davey. "I'm here, sweetie," she said. "That's enough practice for today. You did great. Let's come back tomorrow." Davey sighed in relief.

In the next few days, Davey continued practicing being away from Mom for longer and longer periods. He became good at it and could hold out even if he heard loud noises. He also noticed that Tricksy's stories got quieter. "Great job, Davey!" Mom and Dad said, "but we still have work to do."

"It's time for your next step," Dad said the following morning, and for the next few days, when Davey went to the bathroom, instead of standing where he could see them, his parents let him go by himself, and once in a while, called, "Yoo-Hoo, we're here."

26

Each time he went to the bathroom, they let him be alone for longer. They continued to do that until he spent the whole time in the bathroom all by himself, without a single "Yoo" or "Hoo."

"Let's continue to the next task," Mom said. "Today, I will take you to a friend and leave you two to play alone for a short time." Davey never stayed at a friend's without his parents. "What if something happens while you're gone?" he asked.

"Hey, isn't that Tricksy talking?" Mom asked with a smile. "You will do great, just like you did so far."

Mom and Davey arrived at Davey's friend Kevin. Mom stayed and let the two kids play for a while. Then she told Davey, "I am leaving you two alone, and I'll return soon." And although Davey was scared, he said courageously, "Goodbye, Mom."

Davey held out nicely until thoughts began popping into his head, "Shouldn't Mom have been back by now? Did something happen to her?!" Then, Davey realized something, "It's one of Tricksy's stories!" He continued playing, trying to stay calm.

But as time passed, Davey's concerns grew until he couldn't hold it any longer and heard himself say, "I have to see my mom NOW!" "It's OK. She'll be back soon," Kevin said, but Davey couldn't wait. He had to see his mother immediately, and he burst into tears.

Just as Davey started crying, Mom was back as she promised. Davey rushed to her and held her as tight as he could.

That evening, Davey said to his parents. "I can't do it. It's too hard!" "Sure, you can!" Dad said. "We're taking it step-by-step. Remember, your fears are made of Tricksy's stories. That's all." Davey felt better and decided not to give up.

The next day, Dad took Davey to visit Kevin again. When they arrived, he told Davey, "I will be back soon. You can do it!" Davey took two deep breaths and said to himself, "I will not let Tricksy take over today. Go away, stories!" he roared in confidence.

The boys played with Kevin's toys. After some time, Davey began feeling uneasy, but he bravely overcame it. Suddenly, Davey heard a familiar voice, "Hello, boys!" It was Dad; he was Back. Davey was surprised at how quickly it seemed.

That night, Davey felt thrilled when he went to bed. "I spent the whole afternoon without Mom or Dad!" He thought to himself.

Over the next few days, Davey's parents kept leaving him with Kevin and other friends for longer periods. With each day of practice, Davey felt more comfortable being without Mom and Dad.

After that, Mom and Dad continued to make sure Davey stayed without them as much as possible, and each day Tricksy got quieter while Davey's confidence grew.

Then, on one cold evening, it began snowing. It was the year's first snow. "Tomorrow will be Snowman Morning. Do you think Davey can do it?" Mom asked Dad hopefully. Davey knew what the snow meant. He was afraid but also excited about tomorrow's journey.

The following morning, the children and their parents met at the feet of Tabletop Hill. Davey saw the other children gathering. He looked at his parents, took two deep breaths, said, "Goodbye, I will see you when I'm back," and joined the other children.

After building the snowman with his friends, Davey took a long view from the top of the hill. It was breathtaking. Davey felt as happy and free as he ever did, while back home, Mom and Dad were the proudest parents in town.

Oh, one more thing... Sometimes, Tricksy still tries to put stories into Davey's head, but Davey knows they are just stories, and although being with Mom and Dad is still the thing he loves most; he can freely say goodbye whenever he wishes.

Dr. Jonathan Kushnir
Clinical Psychologist

Dr. Jonathan Kushnir is a clinical psychologist, an expert and an instructor in Cognitive Behavior Therapy, accredited by the European Association for Behavioral Therapies. After completing his Ph.D. in clinical psychology in Israel and a research fellowship in the U.S, he has successfully treated thousands of children and adults suffering from emotional anxieties for over a decade. His insightful articles on the subject have been published in top scientific - peer-reviewed journals.

"The idea for this book series was born after treating numerous children and their parents, and observing their rough and frustrating struggles with anxiety, anger, and sleep disorders. In this book, we aim to deliver the knowledge accumulated over the years in a unique and straightforward way; one that can be easily understood by kids and adults alike."

Manufactured by Amazon.ca
Bolton, ON

40799169R00026